GW00546648

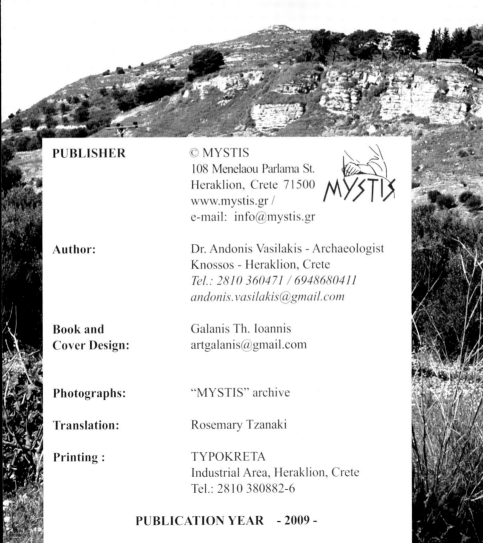

PUBLISHER   © MYSTIS
                         108 Menelaou Parlama St.
                         Heraklion, Crete 71500
                         www.mystis.gr /
                         e-mail: info@mystis.gr

Author: Dr. Andonis Vasilakis - Archaeologist
                         Knossos - Heraklion, Crete
                         Tel.: 2810 360471 / 6948680411
                         andonis.vasilakis@gmail.com

Book and   Galanis Th. Ioannis
Cover Design: artgalanis@gmail.com

Photographs: "MYSTIS" archive

Translation: Rosemary Tzanaki

Printing :   TYPOKRETA
                         Industrial Area, Heraklion, Crete
                         Tel.: 2810 380882-6

PUBLICATION YEAR   - 2009 -

FOREWORD

A new guidebook to Phaistos and the other archaeological sites of south-central Crete is by no means redundant. All the monuments of the Mesara are first-class and testify to the importance of the area throughout history. There has not been a new guide to these monuments for over a decade, while more recent excavations, investigations, studies and publications have added a wealth of information.

MYSTIS Editions and my friend and publisher Andonis Tsindaris have entrusted me with the authorship of a new series of guidebooks on the important archaeological sites and monuments of Crete. We have already published a major guidebook to Crete and a book on Gortyn and its Great Inscription, both written by myself and received enthusiastically by visitors to Crete.

The publisher entrusted the writing of this book on Phaistos and nearby sites to me, as I have studied Phaistos and the other archaeological sites of the Mesara for 30 years and discussed research problems with my colleagues, the excavators of the foreign Schools of Archaeology, whose work I supervised for many years on behalf of the Archaeological Service. The course of our collaboration was smooth and visitors may judge its fruit for themselves.

The photographs were taken, with particular zeal, by Giannis Galanis. The overall editing was undertaken by Andonis Tsindaris, Andonis Vasilakis and the graphic artist Giannis Galanis, who is responsible for the pleasing aesthetic result.

CLARIFICATIONS - INSTRUCTIONS FOR VISITORS

From a turning on the left off the Heraklion - Mires - Tymbaki national road (at the 58th km), a tarmac road winds up the hill of Phaistos. Here, next to the church of Agios Georgios, is an artificial square forming a car and coach park. A cobbled footpath to the east leads to a small square, around which are set the ticket office, the book and card shop, and the refreshment kiosk and tourist shop of the Xenia Phaistos municipal enterprise. The pine grove at the top of the hill, west of the refreshment kiosk,

shades the buildings of the Italian Archaeological Mission at Phaistos, built in the early decades of the 20th century.

At Phaistos, only the enclosed area of the Palace is open to visitors.

The peripheral archaeological sites of Agios Georgios, Agia Photini, Phalangari, Chalara, Agios Ioannis (paved road), Agios Pavlos (Geometric tholos tomb), are accessible on obtaining timely permission from the Archaeological Service. Visitors should be aware that during the hot summer months it is difficult to stay in the Phaistos sun for long, and they should wear hats or stay in the shade of the pine trees for a while. Visitors who have been to Knossos, with Arthur Evans's restorations and reconstructions, will be puzzled at the ruins of Phaistos.

Only the necessary consolidation of fragile sections has been carried out here, and the paved areas mended with concrete or new gypsum from the ancient quarry west of Agia Triada. The ruins of Phaistos are hard to decipher. They need to be explained by a tour guide or the appropriate book. The site guards at Phaistos and Agia Triada are courteous and willing to provide visitors with information.

This book contains a brief overview of the mythology of Phaistos, literary references and travellers' accounts of the site. There is also a summary of the first excavations, the old excavations from 1950 onwards, and the recent excavations of the past 30 years, as well as the consolidation, reconstruction and layout of the ruins.

A short historical timeline of Phaistos follows, and of course the tour of the Palace itself and the archaeological sites around Phaistos, forming the main part of the book.

The area of Phaistos open to the public is presented in 13 sections indicated by the letters of the alphabet from A to N. The areas, rooms and other sections are numbered 1 to 60. Other guidebooks and the information signs follow different numbering. From my long experience of teaching and giving tours of the site - to groups of expert visitors - I believe that the grouping suggested here will help readers and visitors to gain a better understanding of this very important monument.

On completing the tour of Phaistos, visitors have the chance to see some other important monuments in the environs of the Palace, dating from all periods of history.

These monuments include the church of Agios Georgios Phalandras, the excavations at Chalara, the village of Agios Ioannis with the church of Agios Pavlos and the Geometric tomb, and the Monastery of Kalyviani east of Phaistos.

In this book we present, in addition to Phaistos, the equally important archaeological sites of Agia Triada, Kommos, Kamilari, Pitsidia and Matala.

Agia Triada (entrance fee) and Matala are open to the public, while the others may only be visited by prearranged permission of the Archaeological Service.

The excavation finds from the archaeological sites of the Mesara are housed and displayed in Heraklion Archaeological Museum. In a few years' time the Mesara Archaeological Museum at Gortyn is expected to be built, with modern exhibitions of the finds testifying to the rich cultural continuity of the area.

We hope this book will help visitors to understand the major archaeological sites of the western Mesara.

INTRODUCTION

GEOGRAPHY OF THE MESARA

The general geographical term "Mesara" denotes the geographical, historical and cultural entity of the south-central part of Crete. It is named after the Mesara plain, the largest in Crete. Throughout its history, the Mesara has had particular cultural features within the wider Cretan Greek world.

The Mesara plain lies in the midst of the mountains (*mesos* + *oros* = *Mesaoria* = *Mesara*), bounded on the north by the southern and eastern foothills of Mount Ida (Psiloritis), and on the south by the Asterousia Mountains.

To the west, low hills conceal the Libyan Sea. To the east, far away on the horizon, can be seen the low foothills of Mt Dikte and Dikte itself. The plain is crossed by two rivers and their tributaries.

The rivers divide near the village of Asimi and run in opposite directions: the Geropotamos (the ancient Lethaeus or, according to others, the ancient Malonites), runs west to the Bay of Mesara or Tymbaki, while the Anapodaris (the ancient Catarractes) meets the sea in Dermatos Bay, east of Tsoutsouras. The favourable environment, with a wide variety of natural landscapes, provided ideal conditions for the development of civilisation from a very early date, from the end of the Neolithic period (around the 5th millennium BC) at least.

The northern part of the Mesara is dominated by the southern foothills of Mt Psiloritis (it is also known as Pano Riza, "Upper Foothills") and the largely fertile range extending from Agia Varvara in the west to Arkalochori in the east, dividing the district of Heraklion into north and south.

Its soil is favourable for growing olives - sometimes ancient trees - while there also used to be vineyards for both sultanas and wine, and animal husbandry is widespread.

The central plain of the Mesara is now dominated by olive groves, while in the western part vegetables are grown in greenhouses and outdoors. In this area are the semi-urban centres of Mires, Tymbaki, Asimi, Pyrgos, Charakas and Agioi Deka. On the west coast lies the largest tourist resort, Matala.

The relatively inaccessible southern zone is dominated by the almost barren Asterousia range, suitable only for animal husbandry, with old olive trees in some areas. To the south of the mountains are many inlets.

Outdoor and greenhouse vegetables are grown in the small valleys, while there is also some limited tourist development.

HISTORY

The history of the area goes back six thousand years. The place-name "Phaistos" is Minoan (*pa-i-to* in Minoan Linear B script) and has remained unaltered from 1500 BC to the present day. The Phaistos area used to form part of the administrative district of Kamilari Community, and it is now in the Municipality of Tymbaki in the District of Pyrgiotissa of Heraklion Prefecture.

NEOLITHIC PERIOD

The hill of Phaistos was first inhabited in the Final Neolithic period (4th millennium BC). The Neolithic settlement, which was fairly extensive, covered approximately 50,000 square metres. The houses, built next to each other, were rectangular in plan, with relatively high stone walls and hearths in the clay floors. A round hut excavated to the south of the Central Court of the Palace is visible today. The excavation, which was carried out in many test trenches under the house floors and in the courtyards, brought to light clay pots, a clay female figurine, stone tools, obsidian flakes, a piece of copper and domesticated animal bones. The characteristic handmade, dark grey pottery is either incised or painted with white ochre, forming an early polychromy, the only example dated to such an early period in the Mesara. There are ample scholarly publications on Neolithic Phaistos.

PREPALATIAL PERIOD

During this period, in the Early Bronze Age (Early Minoan, 2nd half of the 4th and 3rd millennium BC), a new, larger settlement was built on the ruins of the houses of the Neolithic settlement. Ruins from the second settlement have been found everywhere: from Agios Georgios to the site of the Italian School buildings and throughout the Palace, even in the Agia Photini and Chalara areas.

Characteristic parts of two houses, rectangular or square in plan, were discovered under the floor of the peristyle in the Northwest Quarter of the Palace. Pottery in contemporary styles was found in the houses. The other excavation finds (obsidian blades, bone awls, clay loomweights, clay tripod cooking-pots) tell us of the inhabitants' activities (everyday needs, handicrafts). There are no final publications on Prepalatial Phaistos.

PROTOPALATIAL PERIOD

The settlement of Phaistos flourished at the end of the Prepalatial period. The accumulation of wealth was evident and the quality of life was high. The population expanded significantly. The rich demonstrated their power by building the Old Palace in c. 2000 BC, with the intention of gaining economic and political control of the fertile Mesara plain and its environs. For Phaistos, this was the peak of its glory. The Palace became the cultural, political and administrative centre of the "dominion of Phaistos", which extended across the southeast districts of modern Rethymnon Prefecture and the southern districts of Heraklion Prefecture.

The city covered an area of approximately 90,000 square metres. Houses of the time, partially preserved, have been discovered at Agia Photini, at Chalara, under the West Court of the Palace, under the Peristyle Court, in the refreshment kiosk area and near Agios Georgios in the parking area. An elongated room has been excavated next to the footpath, with benches along its longer sides and a paved floor, perhaps a meeting-place for a council of elders. The houses have small rooms and are built next to each other. On the peak of the Afendis Christos hill, west of the Palace, stood a small open-air shrine, as fragments of clay animal figurines show.

The Old Palace was built on three levels on the lower east hill, once the hilltop had been levelled and three artificial terraces with retaining walls constructed on its west slope. The retaining wall of the uppermost terrace permitted the creation of the upper West Court, while the theatre steps were built at its base. On the wider, middle, west terrace were arranged the main parts of the Palace: the paved West Court with the Theatre, the paved Central Court, a tripartite shrine and the wings of the Palace. The south section of the East Wing - the façade is preserved with a course of massive ashlars - included storerooms and workshops. Today, an excavated section of the magazines of the First Palace has been filled in, except for two rooms in which three globular Protopalatial pithoi were preserved. In the south part of the West Court, which was supported by a strong retaining wall, were set the circular stone-built granaries ("kouloures").

The third and lowest level was occupied by yet another paved court and the magazines of the First Palace. The Lower Court communicated with the West Court via paved ascending roads. This area - now largely roofed - is not open to the public and may only be visited by experts.

NEOPALATIAL PERIOD

In 1750 or 1700 BC came the great catastrophe by earthquake and fire which struck most of the centres of Crete and shook the economic and political system of the island. At Knossos, the New Palace immediately began to be built on the razed ruins of the old. Reconstruction also began at Phaistos, after the ruins had been filled in under a thick layer of lime mortar, but work was soon discontinued. That was when the Northeast Sector was constructed outside the Palace, and used to house the inhabitants of the Palace while it was being rebuilt. The interruption of building work is interpreted in the light of new evidence on nearby Agia Triada and on Knossos as the capital of the whole of Crete. The new excavations, research and studies at Phaistos and Agia Triada have shown that in the 17th c. BC, the political and administrative centre and the king's residence were transferred to Agia Triada, at the instigation of Knossos. It was there, at Agia Triada, that the splendid Little Palace, also known as the "Royal Villa", was built, and the representative of the new authority installed.

At Phaistos, work on the New Palace was resumed around 1600 BC and completed in the early decades of the 16th c. BC.

The New Palace is 1,000 sq.m. smaller than the old. The west façade was erected 7 m. east of the previous one and 1 m. higher, on the lime-mortar floor.

The West Court was filled in together with the four lowest steps of the Theatre and left unpaved. It is obvious that the New Palace lost its importance, which passed to the palace of Agia Triada. Phaistos retained its religious and economic functions, although the settlement also shrank compared to the Protopalatial area. One megaron has been excavated at Chalara, one at Agia Photini, and a third has been identified at Agios Georgios.

POSTPALATIAL PERIOD

The New Palace of Phaistos was destroyed in 1490/1450 BC, abandoned and never rebuilt. The settlement shrank appreciably in size. A building of the period has been excavated at Chalara, while the tholos tombs with a dromos (passageway) at Kalyvia and Liliana are of the same date. In the 12th century a large house was built to the west of the theatral area. It was formerly believed that a partial "resettlement" had taken place on the site of the ruined Palace of Phaistos, but today this does not seem to be borne out by careful study of the data.

GEOMETRIC AND ARCHAIC PERIOD

After 1100 BC, a fortified residential nucleus arose on the hill-top. A few centuries later, from the 8th c. onwards, there was an important Geometric settlement on the southwest slope of

the hill, west of the Palace, with other, smaller residential districts on the sites of Agia Photini and Chalara. The districts were linked by cobbled roads, one of which has been excavated in the Geometric Quarter.

In the 7th c. BC a large tripartite temple of the goddess Lato (Leto), the mother of Apollo and Artemis, was founded on the south slope, below the West Wing and the Central Court of the ruined palace. (It was formerly referred to as the Temple of the Great Mother - Rhea, and is still occasionally noted as such). A shrine or small temple has been identified on the site of the Italian School storerooms.

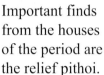

Important finds from the houses of the period are the relief pithoi. An intact tholos tomb of the Geometric period has recently been excavated near the church of Agios Pavlos in the village of Agios Ioannis. A limestone column capital with a Doric echinus (rounded moulding), dated to the 6th c. BC, was discovered on the south slope of the hill. The inscriptions found at Chalara and Agios Ioannis date from the same century. The inscriptions concern legal matters and predate the Great Inscription of Gortyn. The Archaic period of Phaistos is still relatively obscure. It is significant that the theosophist and mage Epimenides, who cleansed Athens of the Curse of Cylon in the early decades of the 6th c. BC, was from Phaistos.

CLASSICAL, HELLENISTIC, GRECO-ROMAN PERIODS

There are gaps in the research on the Classical period (5th-4th c.) It has been suggested that Phaistos was not effectively independent, but under the control of Gortyn, with which it shared its coinage, as a neighbouring community. The city of Phaistos covered a wide area in the Hellenistic period (3rd-1st c.) Houses of this period have been excavated on the site of the ruined palace and all over the hill as far as Agios Georgios.

There was a fortification with towers at the northern foot of the Afendis Christos hill.

A residential district of houses and handicraft installations (weaving workshops) has been excavated at Chalara. An olive mill installation has been brought to light in the Agia Photini district. East of the tarmac road, before the village of Agios Ioannis, a section of a paved road with preserved cart tracks has been excavated, along with the façade of an important Hellenistic house.

A funerary building with dressed stones of the Hellenistic period has been discovered at the "Porous" site, west of Agios Ioannis. During the Hellenistic period, there was also a pottery and vase-painting workshop in the Phaistos area, producing characteristic Hadra ware with brown decoration on a light background.

The city was partially destroyed in the final decades of the 3rd century. However, Phaistos still appears as an independent city in the treaty of the Cretan cities with Eumenes of Pergamon, mentioned third after Gortyn and Knossos.

It was finally destroyed in c. 150 BC by neighbouring Gortyn, according to ancient sources and the excavation finds. The only ruins dating from the Roman period are those of a farmhouse of the 2nd-3rd c. AD in the Chalara district.

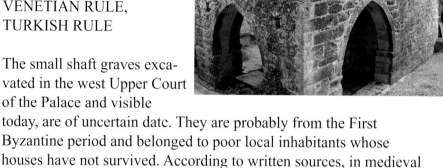

BYZANTINE PERIOD, VENETIAN RULE, TURKISH RULE

The small shaft graves excavated in the west Upper Court
of the Palace and visible
today, are of uncertain date. They are probably from the First
Byzantine period and belonged to poor local inhabitants whose
houses have not survived. According to written sources, in medieval
times the area was known as Melikas.

The missionary St John the Xenos and Hermit, from the nearby
village of Siva, was active throughout Crete in the late 10th century
after its liberation from the Arabs, encouraging the Orthodox faith
of the Cretans. Along with other churches, particularly in west
Crete, he is supposed to have founded those of Agios Georgios
Phalandras and Agios Pavlos in the cemetery of the village of Agios
Ioannis.

MYTHS, CULTS AND COINS OF PHAISTOS

A. MYTHS

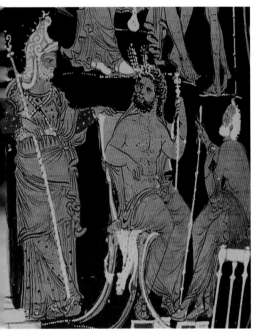

Cretan mythological tradition links Phaistos with glorious legendary figures. According to the oldest tradition, mentioned by Homer and Hesiod, Rhadamanthys, son of Zeus and Europa, was ruler of the Phaistos area, which fell to him when Minos divided the kingdom of Cretas into three. A different myth, however, says that Minos did not share power but, having exiled his other brother Sarpedon to Lycia, made himself monarch, appointing Rhadamanthys "lawgiver" and "judge", to supervise the enforcement of the laws sent by Zeus. In Hades, Rhadamanthys, together with Minos and Aeacus, became the judge of the dead who came from Asia.

He also became famous outside Crete and was sent by Minos to establish justice on the Aegean islands and in Asia Minor. Rhadamanthys set up his own and Ariadne's sons as rulers of the islands and Asia Minor.

We also find him in Boeotia, where he married Alcmene, the mother of Hercules. Rhadamanthys and Palamedes were the inventors of laughter. At Phaistos, the famous "Phaistian laughter" formed part of youths' education.

The eponymous hero of the city was Phaestus, son of Hercules. He is connected to Rhadamanthys and Phaistos in another way, since Rhadamanthys married Alcmene after the death of her husband Amphitryon, becoming the "stepfather" and tutor of Hercules. Rhadamanthys and Phaestus may even have been the same person, in which case the latter name was invented to explain the name of the city.

In another tale, Phaestus was the son of Talos, the son of Cretas and half-brother of Minos. In this genealogy, mentioned by Pausanias, Rhadamanthys was the son of Phaestus. The eponymous hero of Gortyn, Gortys, was Rhadamanthys' son. Rhadamanthys founded Gortyn in order to honour his own and his brothers' birthplace.

2. THE WORSHIP OF LATO PHYTIA, LEUCIPPOS, THE "ECDYSIA"

The deities, mythical figures and heroes worshipped and honoured with festivals at Phaistos were the Pythian Apollo, Artemis, Hercules, Leto Phytia, the Great Mother, Phaestus and Talos. One of the festivals celebrated at Phaistos was the Ecdysia, in honour of Lato (Leto) Phytia. During the festival children passed from childhood into adolescence. The goddess's name is preserved in the Geometric temple founded in her honour south of the palace ruins, and in the rocky islets in the Bay of Mesara, the "Isles of Leto", the modern-day Paximadia.

The origins of the cult of Leto (Lato in the Doric Cretan dialect) appear in the lovely myth of Leucippus. Leucippus was born a girl, but her mother Galatea dressed her as a boy, to deceive her husband Lambros who wanted a male child. When the child grew up it became hard to hide her true sex.

To prevent Lambros from discovering it, Galatea called on the goddess Leto for aid. The goddess "planted" the child ("*phyteuo*", whence the epithet *Phytia*) with male sexual organs. When the time came for Leucippe (now Leucippos) to cast off his childhood garments and wear men's clothes, he was revealed to be a boy, as the goddess had transformed him.

There are variations on this myth; one, by Ovid, says that the child's parents were named Lygdus and Telethusa, and the child was called Iphis after his grandfather (the name Iphis can be either male or female). Lydgus had warned his wife, a worshipper of the goddess Isis, to kill the child if it were a girl. Isis and all her retinue appeared to the mother in a dream and ordered her to keep the child and bring it up, no matter what its sex.

The mother gave the child to a nurse and made sure its sex remained hidden.

When she was thirty years of age, Iphis had a rare, feminine beauty but had to be married, according to tradition. A bride, Ianthe, was found, but the wedding was continually postponed in order to conceal the truth. When the wedding date was set, Telethusa, in desperation, prayed to Isis for aid. When she returned home, the goddess had worked her miracle: Iphis was now a handsome man.

The wedding was celebrated and Iphis kept his promise to the goddess, offering his gifts to her, as recorded in an epigram. After this event, it became a marriage custom for the newly-weds to lie next to the statue of Leucippus, in a symbolic fertility rite.

The festival of the Ecdysia which was held at Phaistos refers to a ritual act, the removal of clothes (*ecdysis*), for fertility purposes. It was also a rite of initiation, for the youth's entry into the adult community. During the initiation, a bull was sacrificed by the initiator, the adult who had taken charge of the adolescent as a "*philetor*". The male garment worn by the youth at the ceremony was also a gift from the initiator. Before putting it on, the youth had to take off his childish garment in order, now an adult, to be able to marry according to the traditions of the city.

3. COINS

The coins of Phaistos - many of them silver - in Classical times bore scenes representing the myths and legendary figures connected to the city. There are seven basic types of city coin from the 5th to the mid-2nd century BC. The two sides depict:
- Europa on the bull, with the bull facing her, or the head of Europa
- The bust of the bull
- Talos as a naked, winged youth
- The young Hercules with his lion skin
- Velchanos
- Phaestus (?)
- Hermes seated on a rock
- A lion

LITERARY TRADITION

Homer refers to Phaistos as a city "fair to dwell in", one of the seven cities of Crete which took part in the Trojan War under Idomeneus.

Phaistos was famous as the birthplace of the mage and theosophist Epimenides, who was active in Athens and Sparta circa 600 BC. The geographer Scylax places Phaistos south of Syvritos (an ancient city in Amari, Rethymnon), while Pliny lists it after Gortyn and before Knossos. Stephen Byzantius calls it a "mainland" city and attributes its foundation to Phaestus, the son of Ropalos, the son of Hercules. According to Pausanias, however, Phaestus was a son of Hercules who came to Crete in fulfilment of a prophecy. The connection of the city to Hercules is also borne out by its coins, some of which depict the hero. The "Isles of Leto", the Paximadia islets off the Bay of Mesara, which were named after the goddess Leto, also belonged to the "Phaestia" or "Phaestiada" territory. The geographer Strabo and the mythographer Diodorus mention the exact location of Phaistos, its foundation by Minos - along with Knossos and Cydonia - and the fact that it was Epimenides' birthplace. Strabo and Eustathius also accurately record its position and distance from Gortyn, the sea and Matala. Strabo writes:

"Of the three cities founded by Minos, the last, which was Phaistos, was razed by the Gortynians. It was 60 stadia distant from Gortyn, 20 from the sea, and from Matalon, the seaport, 40 stadia. The country is held by those who razed the city. Epimenides, who performed purifications by means of his poetry, is said to have been a native of Phaistos. Lisse [the site of Kommos] also belongs to the territory of Phaistos."

Strabo, *Geographica* X.4.14

TRAVELLERS AND EARLY RESEARCH

The first to identify the ruins on the hill of Kastri with the site of ancient Phaistos was the British Captain Spratt, in the mid-19th century, based on the information provided by the geographer Strabo (64 BC - 24 AD) and other ancient authors.

In his book Travels and *Researches in Crete*, based on his visits in 1851-1853, Spratt writes:

"Phaestus, shown by its coins to have been a town of considerable antiquity and importance, and founded by Minos, was said to have been in the vicinity of Metallum [Matala], and, according to Strabo, only twenty stadia from the sea. It was the most important city of the south coast of Crete before Gortyna became the capital; but being early destroyed by the Gortynians, it no longer existed in the days of Strabo, and I was unable to discover or hear of its site on the present mission. But in a journey very recently made from Fair Havens [Kali Limenes], especially to search for it and to revisit Gortyna, I came upon an ancient site at a place called Agia Fotia, situated between the village of Debaki [Tymbaki] and Metropoli or Agious Deka, and agreeing with the distances given by Strabo. I thus found that Phaestus had occupied the extremity of a ridge that divides the maritime plain of Debaki from the plain of the Messara, so as to command the narrow valley of communication between this maritime plain and the inland territory of the Messara, belonging to the Gortynians, and through which the Lethaeus flows to the sea.
The river consequently passes close under the north extremity of the ridge, where it rises into an elevated and precipitous termination, and where there are vestiges still of an acropolis, or its enclosing walls, upon the narrow crest. The acropolis-hill is locally called Kastri. Independently of these remains, vestiges of the old city can also be found in the plain beneath, to the south, in the many fragments of pottery and stones that bestrew the surface of the fields that are now cultivated on the old site, and as far south as the chapel of Agios Ioannis, which is nearly a

mile from the Kastri hill, thus showing the original extent and importance of this early city of Crete."

Captain T.A.B. Spratt, *Travels and Researches in Crete*, II, 2

FIRST EXCAVATIONS

The ruins of Phaistos mentioned by Captain Spratt were identified in 1894 by the Italian archaeologists Federico Halbherr and Antonio

Taramelli. Following the liberation of Crete from the Turks (1898), the Italian School of Archaeology requested and received a permit from the semi-autonomous Cretan State to excavate Phaistos. The excavations began under Federico Halbherr and Luigi Pernier, who discovered the Palace. Luigi Pernier writes in his diary:

"Saturday, 3 June 1900. At 9 we set out from Agioi Deka for Mires and Phaistos. At 11 we reach Phalandra, the height on which Phaistos stood, at the abandoned monastery. Beyond the Lethaeus to the north is Vori, to the south Agios Ioannis - two tiny villages ravaged by malaria. Setting up camp takes until 5 in the afternoon. We will stay in the monks' cells to the west, and we set up the tents between the church and the north side."

(Diary of Luigi Pernier, excavator of Phaistos, from a Greek translation by V. La Rosa)

Three months later, Federico Halbherr wrote to his patron, the academician and senator Domenico Comparetti:

"3 September 1900. Your Excellency, I spent almost the whole summer in the Mesara working at Phaistos, Gortyn and Lebena... The best news is from Phaistos, where we discovered the Mycenaean Palace - a building of enormous dimensions which will take at least two or three seasons to excavate fully. Dr. Pernier, whom I have left to continue the work, will stay until the end of September. Because the area suffers from malaria, we must interrupt the excavation then and recommence in the winter. The palace at Phaistos, of which more than a third has come to light, has produced beautiful Mycenaean vases, clay figurines, like those of Troy, animal figurines, two exceptional offering vessels with spiral relief decoration similar to that of the stele from Mycenae, fragments of painted plaster, bronzes, etc. The palatial complex has signs on stones like those of Knossos, 24 different signs to date, but we have not yet found inscribed tablets, although I hope we will later."

(Letter from Prof. F. Halbherr to academician D. Comparetti)

MODERN EXCAVATIONS

After 1950, the then Director of the Italian School of Archaeology at Athens, Doro Levi, and his colleagues resumed excavation work. They uncovered impressive sections of the Old Palace on the southwest slope of the hill, and parts of the Minoan and Hellenistic town elsewhere. Levi dug test trenches in many places under the floors of the New Palace and confirmed the building sequence of the earlier phases.

He also consolidated and restored parts of the Palace and placed the first roofs over the most vulnerable areas.

In recent decades the Palace and city of Phaistos have been investigated by the Italian Archaeological Mission, under the direction of Professors Vincenzo La Rosa and Filippo Carinci with a team of colleagues, and the Greek Archaeological Service, which is carrying out consolidation and layout work on the ruins. The test excavations have clarified the dating issues arising from Doro Levi's views. In this book, I have followed the more recent views expressed over the last 20 years by Professor Vincenzo La Rosa.

TOUR

A. AREA OF THE UPPER COURT

From the main entrance and the ticket booth, visitors descend to the paved Upper Court. From here there is a magnificent view of Mount Psiloritis, the Mesara plain, the small town of Mires, and the villages of Pombia, Petrokefali, Kousses, Siva, Agios Ioannis and Kamilari. Low on the southern horizon are the Asterousia Mountains. A large part of the Palace is also visible from this court.

UPPER COURT (1)

The Upper Court was first paved in the Protopalatial period. It was used throughout the history of the palace, city and settlement of Phaistos up to the medieval period, as demonstrated by the small, poor shaft graves preserved west of the processional causeway.

The court is crossed by a wide processional causeway running north to south.

Along the west side of the Upper Court, in front of a later drystone wall which is now mostly covered in greenery, there are 17 circular holes in the pavement.

These were for inserting wooden columns, forming a colonnade alongside a wall a little further to the west. This shallow stoa, together with the whole paved Upper Court, is dated to the Protopalatial period.

HELLENISTIC HOUSE (2)

A large building with seven rooms was built on the southwest part of the court in Hellenistic times. The walls were built using ashlars (blocks of dressed masonry) and the stones of the Upper Court which were situated here. The floor of the west rooms is the natural bedrock. Due to its size and location, this house may have been a public hall, perhaps the Andreion (or Prytaneion) of the Hellenistic city. The largest rectangular room has two bases for columns supporting the roof and a central, built, rectangular hearth.

A low stone bench runs around the walls, while the entrance was in the south long wall. The doorways of the rooms have monolithic jambs. The two small south rooms were auxiliary rooms.

NORTH STAIRCASE (3)

Visitors descend into the middle West Court by a wide staircase with 20 steps. The staircase (according to one theory) was built at the start of the Neopalatial period, but the first excavators believed it to be contemporary with the Upper Court and West Court, dating from the Protopalatial period but continuing in use in the time of the New Palace. The rock of the west Upper Court had been deeply excavated for its construction. High up to the east of the stair is preserved a large stone thought to be the base of a wooden column, leading some scholars to believe that the Upper Court had a colonnade and stoa on this side too. The last step is set on the carved rock and connects the Upper Court to the West Court of the New Palace, which had an earth floor.

B. AREA OF THE WEST COURT

The area of the West Court (6) is the most fascinating part of the
Palace and indeed the entire site, as it offers a clear view of many
areas, some of which are currently off limits to visitors. It is
bounded on the north by a well-built retaining wall of ashlar
masonry - restored after excavation - which also forms the wall of
the "Theatre" with its eight wide steps. This wall supported the
Upper Court, which was on a higher level, and dates from the time
of the New Palace, although the foundations of a similar
Protopalatial wall were found just a little further forward.
The West Court was bounded on the west by an enclosure whose
foundations have been discovered. To the west of the court
extended the west Protopalatial district of the Minoan city, as well
as the districts of later periods of the city at higher levels. To the
south lay the Lower Court, a large part of the ruins of the Old
Palace, districts of the Minoan city, the ramps connecting the Lower
to the middle West Court, the Geometric Quarter of the city and the
Temple of Leto (or Rhea).
To the east of the West Court is the bottom part of the Old Palace
façade, the east side of the West Court of the New Palace, and the
partially-reconstructed façade of the New Palace. To the south, the
court was bounded by a solid retaining wall, within which the round
kouloures had been built.
Test excavations in the southwest part of the paved West Court
showed that there were two older paved floors, corresponding to the
two earlier phases of the Old Palace.

SHRINE (4)

As soon as visitors descend to the northeast corner of the West Court of the New Palace, they see before them, on a lower level, the ruins of a small Protopalatial shrine. The shine, which probably had a tripartite façade and was higher in the centre, consisted of three small rooms with thin walls on the side of the courtyard and two larger rooms with thick walls at the back. The finds from the building identified it as a shrine. In the large inner room, on the side of the Great Staircase, there was a low kernos or offering table on the floor, with a depression in the centre for collecting the liquid from offerings. A triton shell also found here was used as a ritual vessel. In the next room was a quern for grinding grain and a unique stone vessel with incised doves. In the small front room on the north there is a low bench with a slab for grinding grain and a cavity for collecting the flour, which was used in offerings. There is another low bench in the middle small room, along with a square stone basin.

The other finds from the small rooms were offering tables, stone vessels and fruit bowls.

To the northwest of the shrine, in a small open area carved into the rock in front of the two staircases, there is a carved niche which served as the sacrificial altar, as it was full of animal bones, ashes and sherds from Kamares pots.

THEATRE (5)

The theatral area was constructed in the time of the Old Palace and is as magnificent as that of Knossos - which, however, is Neopalatial in date. The retaining wall of the Upper Court, with its indentations and slight pyramidal inclination upwards, served as a sort of amplifying device for the ceremonies held in the paved courtyard.

Eight wide steps formed the seats of the audience. In the time of the New Palace, four of the eight steps were covered over and the new floor of the court was made of earth; according to one theory, this meant that it could be used for bull-leaping.

On the east can be seen the lowest course of the façade of the second phase of the Old Palace.

In the right light, the chisel marks on the orthostats are still visible.

This façade, together with the shrine and the four lowest steps of the theatre, was coated with a thick layer of lime mortar in preparation for the construction of the New Palace.

The new façade was built further to the east. As the capacity of the theatre was reduced during the New Palace period, spectators could have watched from the Upper Court, the North Staircase and the imposing wide staircase, as well as from the windows and verandas of the west façade of the palace.

PROCESSIONAL CAUSEWAYS (7)

The paved West Court is crossed by two processional causeways.
The first, wide and magnificent and running roughly north to
south, starts at the theatre steps, crosses the court, turns east past
the southwest corner of the façade of the Old Palace and leads to
the propylon (porch) of the same palace. The second causeway,
which is narrower and runs east to west, starts from the southwest
corner of the court, where the Protopalatial ramps ended, passes
in front of the two westernmost "kouloures" and meets the main
processional
causeway.

NORTHWEST QUARTER - KILN (8)

West of the court you can see the ruins of houses dating from the Protopalatial and later periods.
These ruins are visible from the West Court but are not currently open to the public.
Right next to the theatre and west of it is a small, partially-preserved building dated to the so-called "transitional" period, after the destruction of the Old Palace and before the foundation of the new.
On a higher level a Hellenistic house has been excavated, with a characteristic central room containing a central built hearth and bases for wooden columns.
Among the ruins of the houses of the Protopalatial west quarter, a Neopalatial potter's kiln has come to light, with a small paved area south of it.
The kiln is tear-shaped with the narrow end to the south. It has three small firing chambers separated by low clay walls. It was found in good condition and is protected by a temporary roof.

"KOULOURES" (9)

On the south side of the West Court are
the four circular stone-built structures
known as "kouloures" (rings). They are
usually interpreted as granaries but also
as water cisterns or rubbish dumps,
because they were found to contain
animal bones, ashes and stone tools.
Between the two western kouloures and higher up is the coping
of a cistern dating to the Hellenistic period. The kouloures
were used in both the Protopalatial and Neopalatial periods.
The second kouloura from the west has been partly covered by
the cobbled road built in Historic times. South of the two
eastern kouloures is preserved a large section of the rough
retaining wall of the Protopalatial West Court, with four empty
spaces.

Γ. AREA SOUTH OF THE WEST COURT

The fenced area south of the West Court, currently off limits to visitors, includes the cobbled road of the Geometric period and the Geometric Quarter, the narrow paved ascending ramp (three consecutive phases) connecting the South Court to the West Court, the paved Lower Court of the Old Palace, the roofed ruins of part of the Old Palace, and the Archaic Temple of Leto (or the Great Mother).

COBBLED ROAD (10)

In a higher stratum, above the Lower Court, lay the Geometric Quarter of the city. It was bounded on the west by a wide, ascending, cobbled road, running from the city, to the southwest, and ending in the West Court. The road is made of small and medium-sized slabs. Part of this road, which was used for about 500 years, was discovered in the former Georgios Glambedakis plot, before the village of Agios Ioannis.

RAMPS OF THE PROTOPALATIAL PERIOD (11)

There ramps, which follow the inclination of the slope, are narrow, ascending, paved roads belonging to the three successive phases of the Old Palace.
They ran northwest from the Lower Court - today they are under the cobbled road - before turning west and north again to end in the West
Court.

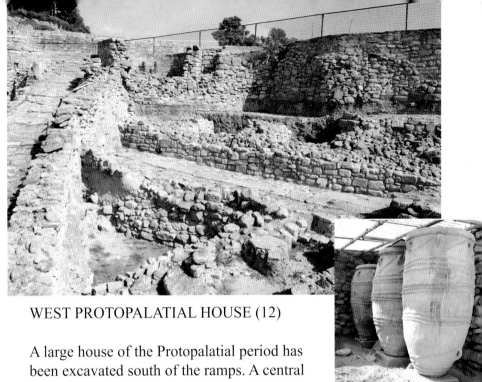

WEST PROTOPALATIAL HOUSE (12)

A large house of the Protopalatial period has
been excavated south of the ramps. A central
room contains a magazine of large pithos jars
protected by a temporary roof.(13) The pithoi
are decorated with bands of rope motifs in relief and paint
splashed randomly over the body. They have carrying handles
below the rim and low down on the body.

LOWER COURT (15)

The paved Lower Court is dated to the earliest phase of the Old
Palace period. The façade of ashlar orthostats is preserved, with
the indentations and protrusions common in façades. On the
north side of the court is a
"bastion" or tower-like structure
supporting a sloping "ramp"
which ran east   before turning
west and up to the West Court.

RUINS OF THE OLD PALACE (16)

This is a large section of the Old Palace - part of the ashlar façade remains - which is preserved to a fairly great height (up to 6 m.), on three storeys belonging to two phases of the Palace: the lower floor corresponds to the older phase and the upper floor, with elements of two storeys, belongs to the second.

This sector is difficult to interpret.

A doorway with three steps leads to a paved antechamber with benches and then into small communicating rooms used as storage areas.

In the walls are cupboards in which, as on the floor, were found beautiful polychrome Kamares pots and various other vessels. On the south side is preserved a propylon and a monumental staircase.

GEOMETRIC QUARTER (14)

These houses are spacious and well constructed, with central stone-built rectangular or circular hearths. Among them is a round pottery kiln. The houses are square, rectangular or irregular in plan, usually have a central rectangular hearth and contained pithoi.

TEMPLE OF LETO (17)

The temple is at a lower level than the Central Court, south of the south sector of the West Wing. It is also visible from the solitary pine tree at the south end of the court. The first excavators believed it to be a temple of Rhea, the Great Mother. The test excavation showed that the temple was founded in the late 7th century. A recent hypothesis proposes it to be the temple of Lato (Leto), the mother of the gods Apollo and Artemis.
It is an elongated, tripartite building with solid walls of dressed stone. The excavation of the temple produced fragments of bronze lebes and shields with motifs in the "Orientalizing" style (naked goddess, deer, etc.) and beautiful pithoi with relief decoration.

Δ. PROPYLON AND CORRIDOR

After touring the ruins of the Old Palace and the Temple of Leto, visitors should return along the cobbled road to the northeast corner of the West Court, where the Propylon of the Old Palace and the access corridor of the New Palace once stood.

PROPYLON OF THE OLD PALACE (18)

The Propylon, or porch, of the Old Palace was truly monumental, as we can see from a surviving column base. From the north corner of the Propylon a wide, paved, covered road, with a processional causeway down the centre, led to the Central Court of the Palace. The east part of the causeway, which was paved with gypsum slabs, lies under the later structures of the New Palace.

CORRIDOR OF THE NEW PALACE (19)

The corridor of the New Palace was built at a higher level to the north, over the filled-in magazines of the Old Palace.

Midway along the north side of the corridor is a room which was used as a guardroom, while another room nearby connected the corridor to the magazines.

OLD PALACE PITHOI (20)

North of the Propylon, under a concrete slab accessed by three modern stone steps, are protected three mended pithoi from the magazines of the Old Palace. There is also an installation used for cooking or, more likely, grinding grain, or even a small wine-press: two stones set up parallel to each other and a duct leading to a liquid collector.

This section, together with the shrine described above, are the only parts of the Old Palace which have been preserved and are still visible today on the level of the West Court. The pithoi, almost spherical in shape, are decorated with ropes and bosses or medallions moulded in relief, and have three rows of carrying handles.

E. WEST MAGAZINES

At Phaistos, the West Magazines occupy the central part of the West Wing of the Palace, south of the great Propylon and north of the shrine complex. The magazines are laid out to north and south of a wide corridor which, unlike those at Knossos and Malia, is oriented east to west. In some magazines, stone tools and implements for various purposes had been stored: olive-press grindstones, ashlars with carved masons' marks, etc.

WEST MAGAZINES (21)

A double doorway leads to the corridor of the magazines, which has a central pillar. To north and south on either side are ten two-storey magazines. Liquid goods were stored on the ground floor, and solid goods (grain, etc.) on the upper floor.
The covered magazine in the northwest corner is characteristic. It contains pithoi - one bearing an incised inscription in Linear A - and a small clay stool, on which people stood to draw liquid from the pithoi. A receptacle for catching any spillage was set into the floor. A raised corridor runs between the rows of pithoi.

ANTECHAMBER OF THE MAGAZINES (22)

The antechamber of the magazines is a large hall with two central columns, two pillars and a large column with an oval base, forming four entrances from the Central Court.

Under the paved floor of the hall was discovered a large number of marvellous sealings (seal impressions on clay) from the Old Palace.

PITHOS MAGAZINE OF THE OLD PALACE (23)

On the north side of the antechamber is a room, with its floor at a lower level, belonging to the Old Palace. A door in the north wall, below the floor of the "Throne Room", leads to an Old Palace magazine with three rooms, full of pithoi found in situ. The magazine was filled in when the great Propylaea and the hall of the New Palace were built. Another room to the west was a "lustral basin" or "adyton" of the Old Palace.

Z. SOUTH SECTOR OF THE WEST WING

The south sector of the West Wing includes the shrines and other places of worship, as is the case at Knossos, Malia and Zakros, where the shrines are next to the central palace magazines.

The sector is divided by a curved corridor running north to south, starting from a doorway in the south wall of the corridor connecting the West and South Courts. This corridor divides the sector into east and west sections (24).

The religious character of the west section is indicated by the existence of two "adyta" or "lustral basins" and four rooms of the shrine. In the east section, on the side of the Central Court, are the rooms with benches and the room with the two pillars. West of the pillar room, on a higher level, are preserved the ruins of a house, probably of the Hellenistic period (30).

DOUBLE ROOMS OF THE SHRINE (25)

The two pairs of rooms were entered from the Neopalatial West Court but do not communicate with each other or the east rooms. The finds from these rooms are connected to worship: a stone lamp, many handleless conical cups and three offering tables.

Two female figurines of worshippers were found in the southwest room. These may have been shrines serving ceremonies held in the West Court.

ROOM WITH BENCH AND ALTAR (26)

The doorway to this room opens off the southeast corner of the access corridor to the New Palace and it is open to the Central Court. Anyone wishing to watch the events taking place in the Central Court could sit on the benches along the north and west walls of the room.

The floor is paved with gypsum slabs. Under the seat, the benches have gypsum metopes with decorative horizontal and vertical triglyphs. In the centre of the room stood a small clay offering table with two hollows in the slab forming its upper surface.

ROOM WITH BENCH AND COLUMN (27)

This room has a column between the jambs of the doorway, which opens onto the west stoa of the Central Court. It also contains a bench similar to that in room 26.

NORTH "LUSTRAL BASIN" (29)

From corridor 24, west of the room with the benches, one reaches the shrines with the adyta or lustral basins and their auxiliary areas. This lustral basin is covered by a thin cement roof. The construction of this section is not particularly luxurious, although the door jambs and thresholds were made of gypsum. The walls were not plastered but only coated with clay.

SOUTH "LUSTRAL BASIN" (30)

The south lustral basin is not roofed. To the north are preserved double corridors indicating the existence of stairs to the upper storey. The complex of the shrines with lustral basins is bordered on the west by the façade of the New Palace.

RUINS OF A HELLENISTIC HOUSE (31)

In Hellenistic times, houses were built in the shrine area, their foundations set into the infill of the palace. These ruins have been preserved with modern concrete pillars which support them at the level at which they were discovered during the excavation.

PILLAR ROOM (27)

West of the ruins of the Hellenistic house, on the side of the Central Court, is the room with the two pillars, a type of sacred space also seen in the central shrine of the palaces of Knossos and Malia. South of the Hellenistic house and the pillar room are preserved solid walls forming elongated corridors. The southernmost walls were retaining walls, supporting the level of the West Wing on the south side.

NEOLITHIC HUT (32)

Southwest of the Central Court, at a lower level than the corridor bordering the West Wing on the south, under the pine tree, can be seen a unique "hut", as the excavators called it, of the Neolithic period. It is a circular structure, partly cut into the rock.

This is the only visible remnant of the extensive Neolithic settlement that stood on the hill of Phaistos in the 5th and 4th millennium BC.

H. CENTRAL COURT

Returning from the south section of the Central Court, visitors can inspect the various sides of the Central Court itself. (33)

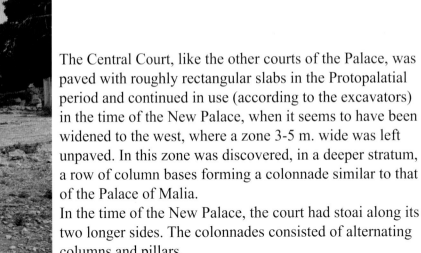

The Central Court, like the other courts of the Palace, was paved with roughly rectangular slabs in the Protopalatial period and continued in use (according to the excavators) in the time of the New Palace, when it seems to have been widened to the west, where a zone 3-5 m. wide was left unpaved. In this zone was discovered, in a deeper stratum, a row of column bases forming a colonnade similar to that of the Palace of Malia.

In the time of the New Palace, the court had stoai along its two longer sides. The colonnades consisted of alternating columns and pillars.

The stylobate (base) of the west colonnade and some column and pillar bases have been preserved in the north half of the court, in front of the magazines.

The stylobate and a row of column and pillar bases of the east colonnade are also preserved on the north side.

On the north, narrow side of the Central Court is the official entrance to the North Court and the Royal Apartments.

The southeast corner of the court may already have collapsed in antiquity.

THE CISTERNS OF PHAISTOS (34)

Characteristic of Phaistos, unlike Knossos, are the many water cisterns dotting the hill. Their presence is due to the fact that there are no water sources in the hills, nor could water easily be piped here from further off and higher up, as at Knossos. The Phaistos water supply was dependent solely on rainwater, which had to be collected in sufficient quantity. L. Pernier and L. Banti write that, "The heights of Phaistos, prior to the Italian excavations, were barren and unhealthy, without trees or water. We reactivated the ancient cisterns..."

The cisterns are located in the Upper Court, the West Court, the south section of the West Wing, the Central Court, the East Wing, the East Court and the North Court.

When discovered, they were all found to be plastered with lime mortar, which dates them to the Hellenistic, Roman and Byzantine periods.

In the testament of St John the Stranger, he says that, "Having climbed the hill, I built Agios Georgios Douvrikas, wherein there is no tree or green grass, but the land is always dry, and I contrived after a fashion to build a cistern to receive the water [rainwater]".

Some of the cisterns repaired by St John the Stranger may be some of those discovered by Pernier when excavating various parts of the Palace.

ALTAR - PITHOI IN THE CENTRAL COURT (35)

In the northwest corner of the Central Court there is a stepped structure which has been interpreted as an altar or an athletics podium.
Here were found ritual vessels of the Postpalatial period, evidence that the altar retained its sanctity.
Next to it are pithoi which, although they have been dated to the period of "reoccupation" and later use of the altar, are dated by their excavators to the Hellenistic period.

Θ. EAST WING

POLYTHYRON HALL (36)

Behind the east stoa, the wing includes a hall with polythyra (pier-and-door partitions), lightwells and a lustral basin. Two small cisterns at the north end of the colonnade are plastered and have a small bench next to them. They may have been used by athletes taking part in competitions held in the Central Court.

LUSTRAL BASIN (37)

Of particular interest is the "lustral basin" in the south part of the wing. The small room was found to contain important

ritual objects: a bull's-head rhyton (libation vessel), two other rhyta in the Marine Style, a jug with a plant motif, a stone bird's-nest

bowl, two stone double horns and a series of votive bronze double axes. From the small room south of the basin came a Postpalatial rhyton in the shape of a human head, a recollection of ancient worship in the area.

"ROCK GARDEN" (38)

A colonnade to the east formed a semi-open-air courtyard, where the rock has remained in its natural state. Holes or depressions have been cut in the rock, while traces of quarrying and ashlar removal remain. The visible depressions have been interpreted, quite persuasively, as a sort of "rock garden" in which flowers were planted.

I. NORTHEAST COURT - WORKSHOP   SECTOR

A doorway in the northeast corner of the Central Court leads to the Northeast Court, which was paved, as we can see from a section preserved to the east. To north and west of this court are the various workshops.

KILN (39)

In the centre of the court are the remains of a horseshoe-shaped metalworker's (coppersmith's) kiln, also described as a potter's kiln (39). Traces of molten metal and glaze are preserved on the walls of the kiln. On the west side of the court are rooms used by the workshop craftsmen (40). A paved, stepped corridor connects the workshop complex to the North Court and the Royal Apartments.

GUARDROOM (41)

On the north side of the Northeast Court is a small room with low seats accessible by steps, which was the guardroom of the east entrance of the Palace. Further north, in the area between the guardroom and the Northeast Complex, there are Minoan and later cisterns cut into the rock.

CISTERN WITH STAIRS (42)

Northeast of the guardroom is a small, elongated room with stairs descending into it on the east and west sides, dated to the Protopalatial and used into Neopalatial period. The room has been interpreted as a water cistern or lavatory, or a ritual area, i.e. a "lustral basin" or "adyton", because a kernos (a stone vessel with depressions for offerings) and part of a pithos were found there.

K. NORTHEAST COMPLEX

The building complex extending across a level area on the northeast hillside, lower than the East Court and outside the Palace limits, is of great interest for the construction history of the New Palace, and also because it was here that a rare find was made: the unique clay Phaistos Disc.

This complex can be divided into two sectors. The west sector (apartments 44-45), which has the same alignment as the Palace, probably belonged to the Palace and was directly linked to the nearby Royal Apartments. The alignment of the east sector, on the contrary (apartments 46-47), suggests that it was an independent building from the outset. These buildings are dated to the final phase of the Old Palace, though they were also used in the early New Palace period (c. 1800-1600 BC). The builders of the New Palace may have lived here.

POTTER'S STOREROOM (43)

This is the easternmost structure on the hill. East of the peristyle are a few rooms, one of which the excavator dubbed the "Potter's Storeroom", because in it were found cups dating from the second half of the 17th century BC, with white decoration, stacked one inside the other.

Two beautiful bull's-head rhyta were discovered in a small corridor with steps.

HOUSE WITH PERISTYLE (44)

The peristyle consists of pillars and columns whose bases have been
preserved.
The floor was
paved with
limestone
outdoors and
alabaster
indoors. The
peristyle was
closed on all
sides, with an
entrance in
the northwest
corner and
another door

and window on the north. The excavator believes that there was
another peristyle with columns on the upper storey. Luisa Banti
considers that the peristyle belongs to a separate house. A
staircase leads from the peristyle up into the East Court and the
guardroom of the east entrance of the Palace.

PILLAR HALL (45)

East of the apartment with the cists is a four-sided room with a pillar in the centre. Here was found a bull-shaped rhyton. The household vessels and tripod cooking pots discovered here led the excavator to interpret it as a kitchen, while the shrine was on the upper storey, and the Phaistos Disc had fallen from there. A small room to the east was a storeroom for household vessels and next to it was the staircase to the upper storey. According to Luisa Banti, the collaborating excavation archaeologist, this building was the house of the palace guards.

BUILDING OF THE CLAY DISC (46)

This unique artefact of the Minoan civilisation was discovered in the small room south of the east end of a row of cists divided by brick partitions. These cists are thought to be sacred treasuries, similar to those of Knossos and Zakros, although no comparable objects were found in them (they may have been looted). The Phaistos Disc was found on the floor of the room along with pottery dated to 1650-1600 BC, ash, coals and burned bovine bones. These finds show that this small, doorless room was a cult depository.

The excavators considered, however, that the disc had fallen from the upper storey, where it was kept. With it was found a tablet inscribed in Linear A, leading scholars to the hypothesis that this was the palace "archive", although it is more probable that its function was religious.

THE PHAISTOS DISC is the most-discussed written text of ancient times. According to L. Pernier, the excavator of Phaistos who discovered it in 1908, it is a representative example of Protopalatial "Hieroglyphic" script. Recent dating of the Phaistos finds, however, has placed the Disc later, in the Neopalatial period, and more precisely, according to L. Godart, in the 16th century, making it contemporary with Linear A script. The clay disc has an inscription arranged in a spiral on both sides. The 242 signs, arranged in 61 groups on both sides of the disc, are images stamped with wooden (or even gold) movable "type" or small seals. The groups contain two to seven signs and are separated by vertical lines which, together with the line of the spiral, form little boxes. There are 45 different signs. The signs on the Disc do not resemble other known symbols, as they have a syllabic phonetic value. It is generally thought that they belong to a script of the same family as the linear scripts. The uniqueness of the Disc - there is no text like it in Crete or elsewhere - makes it a fascinating object, and there have been hundreds of attempted readings. The signs resemble human figures, animals and everyday objects, though some are indeterminate. The contents remain unknown

Λ. NORTH WING, ROYAL APARTMENTS

KING'S MEGARON (47)

This, the most splendid set of apartments in the Palace, consists of a megaron with polythyra in the west section with a stoa on the north, and a covered area with two columns and a lightwell in the east section. The stoa offers a magnificent view to the north, of the valley, the northern hills and Mount Psiloritis. A small room in the northeast corner may have been a sort of guardroom controlling access to the royal megaron. The megaron with the polythyron and the colonnades on north and east are paved with luxurious alabaster slabs laid out in bands with red plaster filling the interstices.

The holes for pivot hinges in the doorjambs show that the polythyron had double-leaved doors. The megaron was decorated with wall paintings depicting ornamental and floral motifs, as the abundant plaster fragments found there prove. A bronze dagger was also discovered in the megaron.

LUSTRAL BASIN (48)

A doorway in the southwest corner of the megaron leads to another luxurious apartment decorated with wall paintings. Here is yet another "lustral basin" with the usual steps descending into it, its walls and floor faced with alabaster slabs, with an attic on the east side. In the west room, an alabaster slab forming a step with a hole and duct has been interpreted as a lavatory (no longer visible today).

QUEEN'S MEGARON (49)

On the west side of the corridor is an attractive hall, usually identified as the ground floor of the "Queen's Megaron". On the west side the floor is paved with "alabaster" slabs, there are benches along the west and south walls, while the walls are faced with alabaster slabs.

On the east side of the hall are two double colonnades opening onto an open-air lightwell with a central rainwater duct and drain. The floor of the lightwell is made of lime mortar.

A doorway in the northwest corner led to a corridor and a staircase to the upper floor.

Another door in the centre of the north wall communicated with the "King's Megaron". A staircase led from the same doorway to the peristyle on a higher level.

NORTH INNER COURT (50)

In the Neopalatial period, this courtyard had a lime-mortar floor. Underneath was the paved limestone floor dating from the period of the Old Palace. It is traversed by an oblique processional causeway, as we can see today.

The Protopalatial court was wider on the west. The building of a palace wall formed an elongated room.

The water cistern with its circular coping, at a higher level, dates from Hellenistic times.

In the northeast corner of the court are two doorways, of which the one with the paved corridor leads to the Northeast Court. From the other one starts the corridor which runs east of the Royal Apart-ments. This corridor is at a higher level than the apartments and is carved into the bedrock.

AREA OF THE PROTOPA-LATIAL PERISTYLE (51)

On the east side of the corridor can be seen the remains of a Protopalatial peristyle with alternating pillars and columns, whose bases are now embedded in the later walls.

NORTH CORRIDOR (52)

The corridor is paved with limestone slabs and has a rainwater drainage duct running along it. At the north end of the corridor is another doorway. The excavators believe that this corridor was partly open to the sky and caught the rainwater, channelling it into the Central Court.

ROOM WITH A CUPBOARD (53)

On the west side of the corridor are rooms with small rectangular wall cupboards, and wall paintings with decorative motifs.

NORTH GATE OF THE CENTRAL COURT (54)

An imposing gateway led from the Central Court to the North Wing. It is ornamented with two half-columns and two niches with wall paintings depicting a row of lozenges. The gate guards stood in the niches. There is a similar niche inside the gateway, at the door to the staircase leading to the upper storey. The threshold has holes for the door pivots and small cavities for a grille.

M. MONUMENTAL PROPYLAEA

After visiting the North Wing, we recommend that visitors return to the corridor of the West Magazines to continue their tour in the north section of the West Wing.

GREAT STAIRCASE (55)

A modern opening in the west wall of the Corridor of the Magazines leads visitors back into the West Court. Passing along the west façade of the New Palace, you come to the majestic staircase, whose 12 wide steps lead up to the monumental Propylaea of the Palace, an entrance consisting of a central column flanked by two pilasters. The staircase is the widest and most splendid found in any Minoan palace. If you examine it carefully, you will see that the centre is higher than the edges, giving the impression that it is curved.

PROPYLAEA AND LIGHTWELL (56)

East of the Great Staircase is a porch with a column, leading to what, judging by its orthostat walls, plaster floor and rainwater duct, was an open lightwell. A staircase on the south led from the lightwell to the upper storey above the magazines, while another entrance on the north led to the stairs connecting the Propylaea to the Upper Court. On the east was a spacious stoa of three columns.

"THRONE ROOM" (57)

The wide stoa has been interpreted as the official "Throne Room" of the Palace. A doorway in the southeast corner communicates with the Peristyle to the north, the magazines to the south and the Central Court to the southeast. Under the concrete floor of the hall is preserved a pithos magazine of the Old Palace.

N. PERISTYLE

From the north corridor, an inner staircase leads up to the area of the four-sided Peristyle.

On the south side is the base of a large column and a corridor also leading to the Peristyle (58).

This impressive space contained large columns forming roofed colonnades on four sides, while the central space was open.

The roofed areas were paved with gypsum slabs. The Peristyle probably had an upper storey with verandas open all the way round, or only on the side of the atrium.

On the north side of the Peristyle is an elongated hall with polythyra, paved with lozenge-shaped gypsum slabs, examples of which survive in the nortwest corner. In the northeast corner of the Peristyle is a doorway leading via a staircase down to the Royal Apartments.

This access is explained by the fact that the area of the Peristyle may have been used as a formal entrance or official banquet hall of the Royal Apartments.

In the southwest corner was found a later bathtub of the "reoccupation" period (1350-1100 BC).

73

PREPALATIAL HOUSES (59)

Parts of rooms belonging to Prepalatial houses have been discovered in the centre of the open area. The pottery found there dates them to the beginning of the Prepalatial period. The walls are well built and the floors were coated with red plaster. It seems that the rooms belonged to two houses of the fairly extensive Prepalatial settlement of Phaistos.

NORTH COURT (60)

On the higher level east of the Upper Court and west of the Peristyle there was probably yet another court, perhaps even with a colonnade on the south side. Many interesting stone tools and architectural members from the whole excavation, including ashlars with incised "mason's marks", have been collected together in the south part of this area.

MONUMENTS AROUND PHAISTOS

MONASTERY OF PANAGIA KALYVIANI

One of the monasteries still active in the Phaistos area is that of Panagia Kalyviani (the Virgin of Kalyvia), a 20th-century building 1.5 km south of Phaistos. Officially recognised as a monastery in 1961, it was originally a pilgrimage site, with the new church built in the early 20th century, the old single-aisled church of the Virgin, the monastery church which was destroyed during the Turkish occupation, and various outbuildings for visitors and monks who had come to live here. In 1956 Timotheos Papoutsakis, Bishop of Gortyn, established the Monastery as a monastic-ecclesiastical foundation with many social activities (an orphanage, an old people's home, a housekeeping school, traditional weaving, ecclesiastical vestments and cutting & sewing workshops, a primary school, a printer's, a museum with an exhibition on local history, etc.)

The old church dates from the 16th century, as evidenced by the wall paintings of the Virgin Platytera (Wider than the Skies) in the bema apse, the Annunciation, Our Lady of the Angels, the Prophets and the Ten Holy Martyrs. Outside the church is a miraculous tree. According to local tradition, the church was abandoned for roughly half a century in 1821 and turned into a stable by the Turks. In 1856 the bema was cleaned out so the church could be opened again. Two Turkish children profaned the church and the Virgin punished them with illness and death. This was considered a miracle, and many worshippers from all over Crete began to gather here for the feast of the Dormition of the Virgin on 15 August, enduring Turkish acts of violence. The issue was settled by the Sublime Porte and the Patriarchate of Constantinople in 1873, when a committee was set up for the management of the rich offerings, the repair of the church, etc. After the miracle-working icon of the Annunciation was discovered under an olive tree, a warden from the Monastery of Hodegetria was appointed in 1875.

AGIOS GEORGIOS "PHALANDRAS"

Of the Orthodox male monastery of Agios Georgios (St George) Ph(a)landras only the church remains, at the west end of the coach park. According to the testament of St John the Stranger, he founded the first church in the late 10th century, but nothing save the water cistern remains to remind us of its early history. The church of the late Venetian period was dedicated, Cornelius tells us, to St George and the Virgin. During the Turkish period, the fortress-type monastery oper-ated as a dependency of Arkadi Monastery. In 1742, according to an inscription on the well   coping, the Byzantine cistern built by St John the Stranger was restored and repaired. The monastery was destroyed in the 1821 Revolution, and at the turn of the 20th century all that remained was the fortified enclosure, the monks' cells to south and west, the south aisle of the church and the defensive tower on the west side of the north aisle. There is also a tomb near the church bearing an inscription dated 1581. The Italian excavators of Phaistos camped here in the summer of 1900. The church is large, with a vaulted roof and few doors and windows. The ogival vault has four supporting arches. An interesting feature is the stone Renaissance icon screen.

"CHALARA"

The "Chalara" district, at the southern foot of the Phaistos hill, has been excavated over an area of 3,500 square metres. The ruins, dating from different periods, are built on terraces. Repeated destructions and the steepness of the slope make them hard to decipher. The area was inhabited from the Neolithic period to the destruction of the city in the mid-2nd century. The centre of the district was reoccupied by a Roman farmhouse in the 2nd-3rd c. AD. The most important finds are those of the Hellenistic period, including house walls of solid, regular construction, courtyards, water cisterns, workshops and paved roads. Of particular interest is a Neopalatial megaron in the south sector, the richest large building of the time discovered in the excavations of recent decades at Phaistos. Near Chalara, in a drainage ditch, a fragment of an Archaic judicial inscription was found by chance in 1978, shedding valuable light on the life of the city in the second half of the 6th century BC. The inscription, in the Doric dialect, refers to a legal act concerning inheritance matters enacted by the citizens' assembly. The inscription is older than the Gortyn Law Code and constitutes an important reference point for the Archaic city of Phaistos, about which little is known.

AGIOS ONOUPHRIOS FIND

Special mention must be made of the group of
finds from Agios Onouphrios, below and
northwest of Phaistos. Discovered in 1894, this is
the first Minoan find said to come from here, even
before the excavation of Knossos. The precise findspot has not
been identified. The pottery discovered here,
decorated with red or brown linear motifs on a
light background, has been named Agios
Onouphrios ware after the small church nearby.
The finds were pottery vessels, marble figurines,
seals, bronze tools, gold jewellery and stone vases.
They most probably came from a looted
Prepalatial tholos tomb, perhaps the large tomb of
neighbouring Agia Triada, excavated by Federico
Halbherr ten years later (1904).

VILLAGE OF AGIOS IOANNIS

The small village of Agios Ioannis, south of Phaistos, is the last habitation remaining in the area where the ancient city of Phaistos once flourished. The village has been here since the Middle Byzantine period, as the church of Agios Pavlos (St Paul) shows. However, in the Early Byzantine period the last inhabitants of Roman Phaistos lived here, around a Christian baptistery on the site known as Loutra, where Agios Pavlos now stands. During the Venetian period the village was recorded as Agios Ioannis of Melikas, a name which also appears in the testament of St John the Stranger.

During the Turkish period this was the home of the bloodthirsty Janissary Agriolidis, whose tower is preserved in the village. Agriolidis terrorised the entire Mesara. The rebel Dimitrios Varouchas or Logios from the village of Agios Thomas died in an attempt to eliminate him in 1811, but in 1828 Agriolidis was killed by the heroes Korakas, Malikoutis and others. In reprisal, the Turks massacred 800 Greeks in Heraklion (the "Slaughter of Agriolidis").

AGIOS PAVLOS

The old church of Agios Pavlos (St Paul), now the village cemetery of Agios Ioannis, is connected to St John the Stranger.

The village itself was actually named after that preacher of the faith from the nearby village of Siva. The dedicatory inscription of 1303 refers to the restoration and rebuilding of the church "on the site of Baptistiras" by the priest Petros and his sister Kataphygi in the time of the Emperor Andronicus Palaeologus. The site of Baptistiras (Baptistery) is Loutra.

The church consists of three parts: the domed bema - the Early Byzantine baptistery; the main church, square in plan with a dome supported by four arches; and the narthex, roofed with a low dome (now a rebuilt traditional flat roof). The dome of the main church has four window slits to let in light.

The wall paintings include scenes from the life of St Paul the Apostle, the Crucifixion, Hell (punishments of the damned), Joachim and Anne, busts of female saints (Ss Marina, Paraskevi, Irene), the Evangelists Matthew and Luke, prophets and a bust of Christ.

The wall paintings of Agios Pavlos and Agios Georgios on the archaeological site of Agia Triada are in the Palaeologue style, and represent the first epigraphically verified evidence of its introduction to Crete.

Characteristics of the new style include the use of supplementary colours in the free portrayal of the faces, the rendering of the volume of the bodies and the lively motion of the figures.

GEOMETRIC
THOLOS TOMB

The tomb was excavated in an olive grove 100 m. from Agios Pavlos, west of the tarmac road to Siva. Its "dromos" (sunken passage) was a ditch dug in the earth. It has a trilith (three-stone) entrance 1.20 m. high and 0.70 m. wide. The tholos has a diameter of 3.23-3.26 m. and a height of 3 m., while the wall was 0.60-0.80 m. thick. A small part of the tholos which had collapsed was rebuilt using the original fallen stones. The tomb, which was full of earth and rubble, contained rich finds; the pottery, in 20 different shapes, is dated from the Geometric to the Hellenistic period, while there was also an iron dagger and other iron and bronze weapons. In the Late Hellenistic period a funerary enceinte was founded over the tholos tomb. It contained two built cist tombs covered with stone slabs, which were found looted.

AGIA TRIADA

After the church of Agios Georgios at the west end of the
Phaistos car park, the road forks. The right-hand fork leads to
Agia Triada and Tymbaki, while the left fork, the main road,
leads to the villages of Agios Ioannis, Kamilari, Kalamaki and
Siva, and on to Hodegetria Monastery and Kali Limenes, or
Pitsidia, Matala and the archaeological site of Kommos.
The archaeological site of Agia Triada, with a view of the
Tymbaki plain and Mount Psiloritis, is on the south bank of the
Geropotamos, at the foot of the last, westernmost hill of the
range beginning at Phaistos, 3 km away. Agia Triada is the
second-largest Minoan site of the West Mesara after Phaistos,
and of equal importance. The ancient place-name is unknown.
It has been proposed that the toponym *pa-i-to* (rendered
"Phaistos"), recorded on tablets in Linear B, corresponds to the
Agia Triada area. This hypothesis is based on the observation
that this was the seat of the kingdom of the Mesara in the
Neopalatial and Third Palace period (17th-13th c. BC).
Other researchers believe that this is the *Da-wo* also recorded
on the tablets.

The modern place-name is that of the small, now-ruined village of the Venetian and Turkish periods to the west of the archaeological site, where the two-aisled church of Agia Triada (the Holy Trinity) now stands. The village was inhabited until the late 19th century and temporarily reoccupied by residents of Tymbaki during the German Occupation. The church of Agios Georgios Galatas, inside the archaeological site, belonged to the village cemetery.

The Minoan palace, the city and the cemeteries were excavated by Federico Halbherr and his colleagues in 1902-1914. Work on the site was interrupted for 60 years. Halbherr was unable to publish the excavation, which was eventually published (the palace only), based on his manuscripts, by his colleague Luisa Banti in 1976.

The following year, Vincenzo La Rosa and his collaborators launched a new period of excavation and study on the excavated site and also in a new sector to the east, with the aim of establishing more accurate dating, reconstructing the stratigraphy and organisation of the site, and finally preparing a new publication, currently in progress.

The ruins are examined here - after a brief history - in three groups: a) the Neopalatial palace and the "megaron" of the Third Palace phase; b) the town, the agora and other megara; c) the cemetery of tholos and rectangular tombs and the Prepalatial district.

HISTORY

The site was inhabited from the beginning of the Prepalatial period (late 4th millennium BC). Parts of the extensive settlement and two tholos tombs were discovered in two sectors: a) in the west part of the excavated area, near the Shrine, where a rubbish dump of the Early Prepalatial period was found; and b) on the north side of the excavation, east of the road running down from the site car park to the riverbed, where the remains are more impressive. They include two houses of the Middle Prepalatial period, with rectangular rooms and one vaulted room. In the centre of the rooms are U-shaped pillars to support the roof. The most interesting finds were the beautiful pithoi decorated with "trickle patterns" and incised or relief ornamentation, and pottery of the Agios Onouphrios and Koumasa styles.

The most imposing monuments of the Prepalatial period are the two tholos tombs. The larger tomb is 9 m. in diameter with a wall 1.80-2.00 m. thick. Its entrance is on the east, with rooms to the south for burials and offerings. It contained about 150 bodies and many grave goods of the Prepalatial and early Protopalatial period. The second tholos tomb, half ruined, is slightly later in date and was reused in the Postpalatial period.

The Protopalatial period (20th-17th c. BC) is not well known. Sections of houses have been excavated in deeper strata in the area of the Shrine, and pottery deposits have also been discovered in various places.

An important feature of the period is the section of a road and paved court in the new northeast sector of the excavation, with an altar and a pottery deposit.

An interesting find was a circular figurine of six female figures with upraised hands, the oldest evidence of this ritual invocation for the epiphany of the deity.

After the destruction of the Old Palace, in the Neopalatial period (17th-15th c. BC), the political situation changed across Crete, with the undisputed domination of Knossos. This resulted in a role reversal for the two centres of the Mesara, Phaistos and Agia Triada. Agia Triada now became the political and administrative centre, where an extensive building programme was implemented from the beginning of the period, including the Palace and megara of luxurious construction to the east.

The relations with Knossos are evident in many features. The Palace is L-shaped, or U-shaped if the west complex is considered to be a part of it.

It is smaller - covering approximately 3,500 square metres - than the other palaces, but its architectural splendour and rich finds make it equally if not more important.

It is often called the "Royal Villa", but it was definitely designed from the outset to play a palatial - and dynamic - part in the Mesara during the Neopalatial period. Its basic function seems to have been palatial, i.e. administrative and economic, in character. Here was found the largest archive of Linear A tablets and sealings in the whole of Crete. The wall paintings (the "Wildcat Hunt") decorating the rooms of the Palace are in the same style as those of Knossos. An important find is the potter's kiln discovered behind the ticket office.

The Third Palace period (15th-13th c. BC) was also a prosperous time for the Minoan centre of Agia Triada. In 1450 BC the New Palace of Phaistos and that of Agia Triada were both destroyed.

For a few decades after the destruction no large structures were
built at Agia Triada, except for an altar in the east sector. After
1400 BC, however, the Neopalatial trend was repeated: Agia
Triada was once more the centre of the Mesara, directly
connected to the new "Mycenaean" dynasty ruling Knossos.
The Linear B archives at Knossos refer to the centre of *pa-i-to*
(Phaistos) and to women and children receiving food rations from
that palace.
The name was applied, from a bureaucratic and administrative
point of view, to both the Agia Triada and the Phaistos area, i.e.
the whole of the Mesara, once the kingdom of the legendary
Rhadamanthys.
The new urban plan of the palatial city contains many
monumental buildings unique for their time anywhere in Crete.
The buildings are divided into two sectors with different
functions. The south sector is located on the site of the ruins of
the Neopalatial Palace. It comprises the palatial Megaron, unique
in Crete, the seat of political authority, and next to it a stoa which
opened onto the paved "Court of the Shrines", at the west end of
which stood an independent shrine with a painted plaster floor
depicting an octopus and dolphins.
The other urban nucleus consisted of the magazines in the Court
of the Agora. A structure 50 m. long, divided into eight rooms
fronted by a stoa, was the state magazines, destroyed
in the mid-13th c.

Two large buildings on the north side of the court, one resembling a megaron and the other with a corridor, had an administrative and economic function and are dated to 1350-1250 BC.

The most important find of the period is the famous stone sarcophagus painted with scenes of a bull being sacrificed to the accompaniment of reed pipes, offerings to the dead, libations and gods in chariots.

All this is evidence of the important historical fact that Agia Triada was the capital of the kingdom of the Mesara in the 14th and the first half of the 13th c. BC.

Following the destruction of the town in 1250 BC, due to the general decline of Knossos and indeed the whole of Crete, only the "Court of the Shrines" continued in use, with open-air depositions of votive figurines.

Worship at the open-air shrine in the "Court of the Shrines" continued into the Protogeometric period (11th and 10th c. BC), and was renewed from the 7th century to the Greco-Roman period. The offerings consisted of human and animal figurines.

In Hellenistic times a small shrine was built over the older one in the court, with another small sanctuary dedicated to the young god Velchanos next to the North Court.

The dedicatory inscription of Arkesilas and roof tiles bearing the god's name have been preserved.

The church of Agios Georgios (St George) Galatas was built in the early 14th c. AD. The village of Agia Triada further to the west was named after the church of the Holy Trinity.

TOUR

The entrance to the enclosed archaeological site is from the car park on the east side. The steps lead down to the ticket office square, which offers a panoramic view of the site: to the west is the Southeast Complex, the "Court of the

Shrines", Agios Georgios Galatas, the ruins of the Minoan palace and over them the palatial Megaron of the third phase. To the east is the "Court of the Agora" and the city of the Neopalatial and Third Palace period. Even further east is the new excavation sector and the tholos tombs.

To make things easier for visitors, we will use a simplified numbering system. Numbers 1-15 are the main sectors and wings of the Neopalatial palace and settlement, the "Court of the Shrines", the Shrine, Agios Georgios and the Sanctuary of Velchanos. The capital   letters A-Δ denote the monuments of the Third Palace period.

NORTHWEST BUILDING, SHRINE, "COURT OF THE SHRINES", AGIOS GEORGIOS (1-4)

A staircase from the ticket office leads to the Northwest Building (1), which some researchers consider to have been independent, but which was probably an annexe of the palace intended for official use, perhaps as dignitaries' residences.

The two-storey building had magazines on the west, and lightwells and stoai on the east side. The cobbled road 12 separates it from the rest of the Palace.

South of Building 1 is the Shrine (2), preserved in the form it took during the Third Palace period. It has an antechamber communicating via two doorways with the cella, which has a high bench against the back wall. The Shrine had a floor of coloured plaster depicting an octopus between dolphins.

East of the "Court of the Shrines" (3) is a cobbled road which may have led to Phaistos. At a lower level, the paved Court was contemporary with the Palace, but in the Third Palace period it was built up higher, paved once more and extended to the north, over the ruins of the palace. To the west is a small court with a two-columned stoa and a small "Theatral Area" with five steps. Here was discovered the "Boxer Vase", a conical rhyton with relief boxing and bull-leaping scenes. The "Court of the Shrines" offers a good view of the palace apartments.

Agios Georgios (4) is a single-aisled church of the 14th century A.D. (1302), according to the inscription which dates the wall paintings, in the Palaeologue style. The church had a stone icon screen set on pillars with an architrave painted with busts of saints. The rich wall paintings depict various scenes including the Officiating Bishops and the Deesis (Christ between the Virgin and St George) in the bema, the Annunciation, the Three Marys (the Myrrh-Bearers), the Ascension and the Presentation of Christ in the Temple.

NEOPALATIAL PALACE (5-11)

The visit to the Palace effectively begins from the northwest, below and west of the church of Agios Georgios, following the paved sea road, which is preserved in some places. The west road 5 starts off south to north, bends east (11), turns south and ends, as stair 12, in the "Court of the Shrines".

Southwest Sector

At a lower level than the court, it consists of small rooms entered on the west from the paved "sea road" (5), while on the east were continuous rooms with windows opening onto corridor - lightwell, which has a drainage system.

The west rooms may have been workshops or shops, and the east rooms may have been storerooms, while some may have been craftsmen's houses.

Another room was a kitchen, as it was found to contain plates with burnt food remains (chickpeas, peas, figs and lamb bones), as well as a tripod cauldron and three pithoi. Other rooms contained two bronze lebes, a bronze hydria and other bronze vessels, a rhyton, tools and loomweights. There were pithoi in the room next to the stairs.

Service rooms (7)

Four rooms, a light-well and a staircase to the upper floor were intended to serve the needs of the official wing which extends to the north. They were used for storing vessels, bronze tools and double axes. One room contained pithoi with incised inscriptions in Linear A.

Northwest wing of official apartments (8)

The official apartments are a network of polythyra, stoai and halls with floors of alabaster slabs with red plaster interstices. The entrance to this complex has not been preserved, but it may have been on the north. The largest room is hall, with polythyra and walls faced with vertical alabaster slabs. On the east are three continuous halls with columns and polythyra. The easternmost room, with benches along three of its walls, contained three stone lamps with a tall foot and the famous Harvester Vase, which had fallen from the upper floor.

The small room has been interpreted as a bedroom. Here were found, fallen from above, clay lamps, a stone lamp with relief decoration, pottery vessels, a bronze female figurine and a bronze box lid with spiral decoration. Area was a stoa whose north and sections have been destroyed, in which were found 179 clay sealings, fragments of wall paintings with floral and linear decoration, an obsidian rhyton in the shape of a triton shell and an alabaster model of a boat, all fallen from the rooms of the upper storey, where the sealing archive was. Another room contained wall paintings and beautiful vases in the Marine and Floral Styles.

North Magazines (9)

Between the official apartments and the magazines are rooms whose use is uncertain, because the palatial Megaron was founded on the site. One room was a storeroom containing 19 copper ingots, while in another room were found bronze male, female and wild goat figurines.

The eight rooms were pithos storerooms.

The magazine complex bears obvious traces of destruction by fire and by the foundation of the palatial Megaron of the subsequent phase.

Some pithoi have incised inscriptions in Linear A. Other finds include Linear A tablets and sealings fallen from the upper floor. One room had a central pillar, but was probably a pithos storeroom, as no signs of worship were found.

Northeast wing of official apartments (10).

These are smaller and were thought to be the women's apartments. They have the typical layout of polythyra, stoai and lightwells. No finds were discovered indicating the use of the apartments. On the west side were the magazines, containing small pithoi, amphorae, stone lamps and a bronze dagger. In another room were found Linear A tablets, pithoi, braziers and ritual vessels.

In front of the three sectors of the Palace described above runs the paved north road (11), a continuation of the west road (5).

The East Staircase (12) links the level of the North Road and the small North Court of the Palace, with the higher level of the "Court of the Shrines".

Palatial Megaron (A)

Also known as the "Mycenaean Megaron". This is a large rectangular building divided into three parts, which was founded on the ruins

of the Neopalatial Megaron in circa 1400 BC. Due to its shape, it has been associated with the new "Mycenaean" dynasts of Knossos.

It has thick walls and covers an area of approximately 500 sq. m. The Megaron was the seat of the kingdom of the Mesara in the Third Palace period. South of the building was a stoa whose column bases have been preserved.

East Stoa (B)

East of the Megaron was a paved road and two drainage ducts, which drained the water from the "Court of the Shrines" to the east. East of the road, over the ruins of the northwest apartments, was built a stoa opening onto the court. Stepped stone bases for double axes were found here, indicating that the stoa may have been a shrine.

North Court of the Palace (10)

The small North Court was accessed by the staircase to the south, was open on the west and had a small pillared stoa on the east. It was used for ceremonies and gatherings. The Sanctuary of Velchanos (10) was established over the east stoa of the court in Hellenistic times. Zeus Velchanos was, in Historic times, a form of the ancient Minoan Young God of vegetation, who died and was reborn each year. At Lyktos the Velchania festival was held in his honour each spring until the 3rd c. AD.

The young god Velchanos is depicted on a silver Phaistos coin standing between tree branches, reminiscent of the union of Zeus and Europa, which is also depicted against a tree.

Neopalatial settlement (14-18)

Our picture of the town in the Neopalatial period has changed following the new excavations.

Bastion (14)

This is a rectangular, elongated building to the north of the court. Its function is uncertain, although it has been interpreted as a fortress. It was used into the next period with a few alterations. Another building, called the "Cyclopean Building" (15) has been excavated on the south side of the court of the stoa. It was used in the 15th and early 14th century, before the Agora was built. Other houses have been excavated in deeper strata. An important example is the "House of the Cauldron" (16), where the finds, apart from a bronze cauldron, included pithoi and large vessels, a clay bathtub and many tablets in Linear A script, demonstrating its close relationship with the Palace.

Other houses with characteristic names are the "House of the Loomweights" (17) and the "House of the Mill" (18). The names indicate their finds and
functions.

AGORA, MEGARA OF THE THIRD PALACE PERIOD (Γ-Δ)

Agora (Γ)

The Court of the Agora was formed in the 14th c. BC, as part of an integrated building programme which also included the Palatial Megaron, its stoa, and a series of megara and megaron-like structures (Δ). All these were built once the ruins of the previous phase had been filled in. The Agora is an elongated building with eight shops and a stoa with pillars and columns to their west. East of the Agora is the East Quarter, where the Necropolis was recently excavated.

In addition to the Palace, two monumental buildings were constructed around a paved area (the new excavation site is not shown on the topographical map), which was used for worship, perhaps funerary, as the cemeteries were nearby. Here, in the new excavation sector, were discovered figurines of a female deity, a stone hammer head and portable altars.

KAMILARI, "GRIGORI KORPHI"

North of the village of Kamilari, on the site known as Grigori Korphi, is the great tholos tomb which was excavated in 1959. It is 7.65 m. in diameter and its wall is preserved to a height of 2 m. It has an entrance on the east, whose threshold was preserved in situ, and seven small rooms. A small court with an enclosure lies to the north of the rooms. The tomb was built in the early Protopalatial period and used more intensively in the 17th c., while it was also used in the Neopalatial and even the Postpalatial period. The finds include dozens of stone and pottery vessels, twenty seals and a variety of jewellery (bronze rings, amulets, necklace beads). Of particular interest are the clay figurines enacting various scenes: a circle dance, making offerings at altars, etc.

KALAMAKI

Monuments of the Minoan period have come to light in the village of Kalamaki, at the site known as Apothestres, along with others from Greco-Roman times elsewhere. A villa with an olive press has been excavated at Sphakoryako.

KOMMOS

The archaeological site of Kommos lies on the beach of Pitsidia, on the site known as "Stou Spanou ta Kefalia", north of Matala, on the Bay of Mesara. The archaeological site has not been built up and preserves an astonishingly strange virginal beauty. The landscape is dominated by the great tamarisk trees on the beach, and kermes oaks, lentiscs, fig trees and vineyards in the sandy interior. Kommos can be reached by a road branching off to the right from the Phaistos-Matala road, shortly after the entrance to Pitsidia, or by another right branch after Pitsidia and before Matala.

The archaeological site was identified by Evans in the early 20th century (1924). The excavation began in 1976 under the auspices of the American School of Classical Studies and directed by Professors Joseph and Maria Shaw of Toronto University, continuing until the 1990s. A large part of the Minoan settlement was uncovered, with large public buildings and a sanctuary complex of the Historic period.

The multi-volume publication of the excavation began in 1995. In recent years there has been work to consolidate the structures and lay out a visitors' route. The site, which is not currently open to the public, includes two major sections of the Minoan settlement, the Minoan public palatial buildings of unique size, and the sanctuary of the Historic period above them. Kommos is one of the most important discoveries of the last 50 years in Crete and the Aegean.

The area was sparsely inhabited in Neolithic and Prepalatial times (3500-2000 BC). In the subsequent Protopalatial period (2000-1700 BC), a sizeable town flourished here. It was destroyed by the great earthquake of 1700 BC and immediately rebuilt. In the Neopalatial (1700-1450 BC), Third Palace and Postpalatial (1450-1200 BC) periods, the town flourished again and spread out to the north and west, outside the expropriated and fenced area.

It has been suggested that this is the "steep rock" mentioned by Homer in the *Odyssey*, on which Menelaus' ship was wrecked on his return home from Troy.

MINOAN TOWN

The excavated sections of the Minoan settlement extend across the side and peak of the low hill of "Stou Spanou ta Kefalia". The settlement flourished in the Protopalatial, Neopalatial and Third Palace period. The first two periods are clearly visible in the part of the excavation on the hillside, where the houses of one period are built on those of the previous one. In the excavated hilltop area, the houses of the Third Palace and Postpalatial period are more obvious.

Narrow paved streets and small paved squares divide the houses into districts. The houses were two-storey, as the preserved staircases show.

Many were found to contain the household equipment and installations, storerooms with many pithoi and vessels, kitchens, a press-bed, stone tools and very important olive press installations.

Some rooms had wall paintings, while much top-quality pottery was also discovered.

On the west side of the settlement there is a narrow cobbled road, running parallel to the beach and leading from the foot of the hill to the houses on the hilltop.

MINOAN PUBLIC BUILDINGS

Kommos was the harbour of the palatial centres of Phaistos and Agia Triada from approximately 1700 to 1200 BC. The large public buildings were discovered low down near the beach, under the sanctuary of the Historic period. The first large Neopalatial building is a sort of palace with a central court and stoai on the north and south, and long, narrow rooms to east and west.

These are shipsheds, used for building, repairing and storing ships. In the 14th century (Third Palace period), a similar, equally large palatial building, of the same date as the palatial Megaron at Agia Triada, was constructed on the ruins of the palace. Here is the start of a wide, paved avenue which probably led to Phaistos, of which Kommos was the main seaport.

SANCTUARY OF THE HISTORIC PERIOD

Founded in the 10th c. BC, this is a rectangular building open on the east with a stone bench against the south wall. In 800 BC another temple was built upon its ruins, containing a central hearth and three small pillars between which were found Egyptian faience figurines, clay and bronze animal figurines and a bronze shield. This sanctuary is evidence of a significant Phoenician influence in Crete in the 8th and 7th centuries BC. A third temple was founded on the ruins of the previous ones in the early 4th c. BC, and its own ruins are visible today. The cella (main chamber) was rectangular in shape with benches running round each side. On the west, the bench was higher, serving as a base for statues (perhaps of Zeus and Athena). In the centre is a rectangular hearth and two column bases to support the gabled roof of the temple. Next to the sanctuary was built yet another rectangular structure with benches which was used as a banquet hall, another for the priests and a round building.

In front of the east side of the sanctuary was a court with four rectangular built altars.

PITSIDIA

MINOAN VILLA AT "PLAKES"

North of the village of Pitsidia has been excavated a Minoan Neopalatial two-storey villa with 20 rooms, corridors, small paved courts and other areas. The outer walls are thick and built of large stones, while the inner walls are thinner and constructed of pebbles and mud. The door jambs were of gypsum. The building was destroyed by an earthquake and abandoned in circa 1450 BC. The finds were pithoi and typical pottery of the Neopalatial period, with an interesting potter's wheel installation.

MATALA

ROMAN HARBOUR AND CEMETERY

You reach Matala by passing through the small town of Mires and the villages of Petrokefali and Pitsidia. There is also a route through the small town of Tymbaki, Phaistos and the villages of Agios Ioannis and Pitsidia. The famous tourist resort is now, together with Pitsidia, a Municipal District of Tymbaki Municipality.

Matala was first inhabited in Hellenistic times, as tombs dating from the period have been discovered at Phournoplago, on the south slope of the mountain bordering the valley to the north. There are ancient references to the city of Matalon, an ally of Phaistos.

This was the main harbour of the capital, Gortyn, from the Greco-Roman to the Early Byzantine period. Parts of the harbour are visible when there is flooding on the beach at the mouth of the river. Many buildings, mainly houses and workshops, of the Roman and Early Byzantine period have come to light on many plots of land in the modern tourist resort. These ancient structures are not visible today, having been buried under modern buildings.

On the south side of the small bay are preserved large fishtanks and shipsheds, in which ships were built and repaired in Greco-Roman times, carved out of the rock.

The most impressive sight is the cemetery on the north side of the bay. It contains chamber tombs cut out of the rock, with beds for laying out the dead, cists and arched niches (arcosolia), dating from the Roman and Early Byzantine period.

At the south foot of Kastri hill is preserved the cave church of Panagia (the Virgin). On Kastri there are Early Byzantine fortifications and many carved water cisterns.

Important remains of a large Early Christian basilica have been found at the site known as Goula, in the village, but the location of the basilica itself remains unknown. Matala gained international fame in the Sixties, when it was popular with "Flower Children".

When the hippies left in the late 1970s, the village rapidly developed into a tourist resort with large luxury hotels, dozens of rooms for rent and many shops for all classes of tourist.

GLOSSARY

adyton (or lustral basin): a special religious space with steps in Minoan palaces and megara.

Agios Onouphrios Style: Early Prepalatial pottery and vase-painting style with brown or red linear decoration.

agora: the central square of a town, around which were established political, financial, athletic and religious buildings.

ashlar: masonry made of large square-cut stones, generally used as a facing material.

Barbotine Style: a Late Prepalatial pottery and vase-painting style with relief decoration on the surface of the vase.

bema: a raised platform at the east end of Orthodox churches where the altar is, forming part of the apse.

cella: the inner chamber of a temple.

chamber tomb: a type of tomb with smooth walls cut into soft rock, mainly in the Minoan, Hellenistic and Roman period in Crete.

cist: a rectangular structure on a wall or floor, for burying the dead or storing objects.

coping: the mouth or upper part of a well.

Doric echinus : a curved circular cornice supporting the abacus (top slab) of a Doric column capital.

double horns (horns of consecration): Minoan religious symbol representing the horns of a bull.

faience: a material used to make figurines and jewellery. It consists of sand, quartz, soda and lime. It is usually varnished and is green-yellow or yellow-white in colour.

figurine: a small statuette representing a human, animal or plant, made of various materials: clay, metal, bone, stone, etc.

Floral Style: Neopalatial pottery and vase-painting style with floral decorative motifs.

fruit bowl: a shape of vessel with a wide, open bowl on a tall foot, used for offering fruit.

Hadra Ware: a vase-painting style of the 3rd c. BC, named after the Hadra Cemetery of Alexandria, used on funerary amphoras and hydriae. Dark decoration on a light background or polychrome decoration on white slip.

Hieroglyphic Script: the first writing of Minoan Crete, created at the end of the Prepalatial period and used in the Protopalatial period. Its name is due to a supposed similarity to Egyptian hieroglyphics. The correct term is Ideogrammatic or Pictorial Script.

hydria: a three-handled water jug.

Kamares Style: Protopalatial pottery and vase-painting style with polychrome decoration. The name is derived from the Kamares Cave on Mt Ida, where vessels of this style were first found.

kernos (or offering table): a stone or clay vessel with many cavities in its surface for offering firstfruits, the first product of the harvest.

lebes: a deep bowl or cauldron.

libation: ritual act in which liquid was poured from a libation vessel onto the earth as an offering to the gods.

lightwell: an area in a building left open to the sky, to provide light to inner apartments.

lime mortar: a mixture of water, lime, ground potsherds and sand, used to make floors or waterproof lining.

Linear A: the system of syllabic writing used in the Neopalatial period in Crete and the Aegean.

Linear B: the system of syllabic writing used in the Creto-Mycenaean period, and in which the Greek language was first written at Knossos.

lustral basin: see **adyton**

magazine: a storage area.

Marine Style: Neopalatial pottery and vase-painting style with decorative motifs inspired by the sea (fish, seaweed, octopuses, etc.)

mason's mark: incised mark on dressed stones in palaces and megara, cut by masons as building instructions.

megaron: a great hall, a rectangular official building with a porch and central hearth.

neighbouring community: a large village near a town or city.

obsidian: a hard, volcanic, vitreous rock with a shiny black colour, suitable for making blades.

offering table: see **kernos**

orthostat: a stone slab set upright at the base of a wall.

Palaeologue Style: Byzantine painting of the 14th and 15th c.

peristyle: a colonnade in a building and the stoa formed by it.

pillar: a square column.

pithos: a large clay storage jar for grain or liquids.

polythyron: (Minoan architecture) an official hall with many doorways divided by piers (pier-and-door partitions). Combined with stoai and lightwells.

processional causeway: a narrow and slightly raised cobbled road crossing a court or a wider road, along which processions passed.

propylaea: see **propylon**

propylon (or propylaea): a monumental roofed entrance or porch of a building, usually with two columns.

retaining wall: a solid wall supporting artificial terraces on sloping ground.

rhyton: a libation vessel, a container used for pouring liquid offerings.

rural villa: a large house of the Minoan and Roman periods with workshop installations and storerooms.

shaft grave (or pit grave): a grave in the form of a simple pit without built walls.

sherd: a fragment of pottery.

stoa: a covered walkway or portico with columns.

theatre: (Minoan) a specially-constructed open-air space in the official court of palaces, with steps for spectators watching ceremonies.

theosophist: an outstanding figure between myth and history, with special gifts and abilities, a theologian, magician, prophet and purifier.

tholos: a dome, a curved part of a building in the shape of a hemisphere, a section of a sphere or a hemicylinder. A tholos tomb (or beehive tomb) is a domed burial structure.

trickle pattern: decoration with brown irregular vertical lines, especially on pithoi.

CHRONOLOGICAL TABLE OF CRETAN HISTORY

LOWER PLEISTOCENE	1.5-0.7 MILLION YEARS BEFORE PRESENT
MIDDLE PLEISTOCENE	700,000-130,000 YEARS BEFORE PRESENT
UPPER PLEISTOCENE	130,000-12,000 YEARS BEFORE PRESENT
HOLOCENE	12,000-9,000 YEARS BEFORE PRESENT

PREHISTORY (BC)
NEOLITHIC

PRECERAMIC AND EARLY	7000-5900
MIDDLE	5900-5300
LATE	5300-4900
FINAL NEOLITHIC	4900-3200

BRONZE AGE - MINOAN PERIOD

		low dating	HIGH DATING
PREPALATIAL	Early Minoan I	3200-2700	
	Early Minoan II	2700-2200	
	Early Minoan III	2300-2100/2000	
	Middle Minoan IA	2000-1900	2100-2000
PROTOPALATIAL	Middle Minoan IB	1900-1800	2000-1900
	Middle Minoan II	1800-1700	1900-1800
	Middle Minoan IIIA	1700-1650	1800-1750
NEOPALATIAL	Middle Minoan IIIB	1650-1600	1750-1650
	Late Minoan IA	1600-1500	1650-1580
		THERA 1520	THERA 1620
THIRD PALACE	Late Minoan IB	1500-1430	1580-1490
(MYCENAEAN)	Late Minoan II	1430-1390	1490-1430
	Late Minoan IIIA1	1390-1360	1430-1370
	Late Minoan IIA2	1370-1320	
POSTPALATIAL	Late Minoan IIIB	1320-1190	
	Late Minoan IIIC	1190-1100	
	Subminoan	1100-1000	

HISTORIC TIMES - ANTIQUITY (BC)

EARLY IRON AGE	Protogeometric	1000-900
	Geometric	900-700
	Orientalizing - Daedalic	700-630
	Archaic	630-490
CLASSICAL		490-323
HELLENISTIC		323-67 BC
ROMAN		67 BC.-330 AD

MEDIEVAL PERIOD (AD)

EARLY BYZANTINE	330-824
ARAB RULE	824-961
MIDDLE BYZANTINE	961-1204
VENETIAN RULE	1204-1669

MODERN TIMES

TURKISH RULE	1669-1898
CRETAN STATE	1898-1913

NOTE :The dates are approximate and are those generally accepted by most scholars today (2009). The columns marked "Low" and "High" dating for the years 2100-1370 BC refer to the two main strands of thought: the older, once-dominant view, still accepted by many; and the more recent view, which also has major supporters, including the author of this book.